Making the most of CHRISTMAS 2

Contents

OUT AND ABOUT

➤ *SHOPPERS' CAROL SERVICE*

This idea comes from a city-centre church. Hold an outsider-friendly all-age carol service at a time when the shops are busy. People should be glad of the opportunity to take an hour off from the hassle of last-minute Christmas shopping.

Hints from experience

1. Timing is important. The Saturday before Christmas and 4.30 p.m. on Christmas Eve are both good times, the latter particularly so – it's when the end of the rush is nigh and the 'magic' starts to break through the madness.
2. Use simple, attractive publicity. Make sure it's free of 'churchy' jargon.
3. Contact local press and radio. See pages 4-5 for further suggestions on successful publicity.
4. Produce a service sheet which includes all of the carols and responses. Include brief details of other Christmas events and provide a contact phone number.
5. Organize distribution of refreshments in a smooth production line.
6. Be as visual in presentation as possible. People are more used to seeing than to listening.
7. Less is more. Compile the service in 'sound-bite' form – lots of small, short items (including the talk!).
8. Keep the pace going. Try to balance the fun moments with several short, reflective, peaceful moments.
9. Be child-friendly without being entirely child-orientated. Singles will come as well as families.

Service outline

Welcome
Short introductory piece of music while candles are distributed.

Responsive praise
The people who walked in darkness
Have seen a great light.
For to us a child is born,
To us a son is given,
His name will be called wonderful counsellor, mighty God,
The everlasting Father, the Prince of Peace.
Glory to God in the highest,

And peace to his people on earth.

Carol: Hark the herald angels sing

Lighting of candles
After lighting the first candle, take it to the start of each row of the congregation and let people pass the flame on. Use the following responses while the candles are being lit:

Jesus Christ is the light of the world,
A light no darkness can quench.
The shepherds kept watch by night
And your glory shone around them.
The darkness is not dark to you,
The night is as bright as the day.
Let your light scatter the darkness
And light up the world with your glory.

Carol: Away in a manger
Bible reading: Matthew 1:18-22
Carol: While shepherds watched
Poem, monologue or sketch
Carol: Angels from the realms of glory
Talk
Carol: O little town of Bethlehem
Prayers, ending with the Lord's Prayer
Carol: Oh come, all ye faithful
Blessing

► *OPENING TIME*

Mark Smith, CPAS Regional Consultant for north-east England, believes Christmas is opening time for the gospel. Here he encourages house groups to take a break from their studies and head for the local.

I've long questioned the value of traditional carol-singing under street-corner lamp-posts. Apart from being very cold, it involves minimal human contact.

Acknowledging that Christmas is one of the most evangelism-friendly times of year, we decided that the best place for our carol-singing would be our local public house. Early in December I called on all our neighbourhood pubs and asked the landlords if they would let us come and sing a few carols. All of them gave us an enthusiastic welcome.

We found that the best approach was to sing two or three carols in each pub accompanied by guitar, piano, accordion or whatever was available. At some venues we used a backing tape – carol karaoke? After singing we stayed around for a chat and a drink. Consistently we found this was the most profitable time. Customers often recognized their friends and neighbours among the church team and asked, 'How long have you been going to church?' or commented 'I didn't know you were religious.'

Pub pointers

- Don't take too many people. You want to fit into, not dominate, the pub scene. Smaller numbers usually mean better conversations.
- Don't try and visit too many pubs in one night. Two is plenty.
- It simply is not worth going before 9.30 p.m.
- Don't rush – stay long enough to chat.
- It's generally best not to take children on these evenings, but if you do, make sure you have permission from their parents and the landlords. Be prepared for them to be bought gallons of pop and loads of crisps!
- Most pubs are used to occasional collections for charity. You may want to avoid reinforcing the impression that the church is always after money. However, I've found that the best conversations and the warmest welcome have been when we have collected for a 'third-party' charity such as Tear Fund or the Children's Society.
- If the landlord agrees, distribute attractively produced publicity for your Christmas services and special events.

➤ # *HOLD THE FRONT PAGE – CHRISTMAS PUBLICITY*

Whatever your Christmas plans, it's important to publicize them. The following check-list shows how easy it is to get your carol service, outreach event or seeker service covered by your local press or radio. Taking the trouble to organize coverage of your Christmas events could be the start of a useful ongoing relationship with the local media.

Eight top tips

1. You are good news for your local paper or radio station. They are looking for stories and contacts, so think how you might interest them and provide the material they need.
2. Do some research before you approach them. Get to know your local papers/radio stations – including free papers, county magazines and independent radio. What kind of stories do they cover? Do they have regular church news? On radio, is there a religious programme? In the papers, an events diary? Think who you might contact (religious affairs editor/producer, local events editor/producer) and find out their names.
3. Think about developing an ongoing relationship with the paper or radio station. Would they like to hear news from you regularly? In what form would they like it – parish magazine, phone call once a month, press release before special events? What is their time scale?
4. Now think of the event you would like them to feature. Do you want them to advertise it before it happens so that people will come, or feature it afterwards with a photo so people get

to know about your church? Could the paper come and take pictures at your event? Can you offer someone articulate to do a radio interview? Think through your approach.

5. Find an interesting angle. Is your church the oldest in the county? An ecumenical experiment? Do you have open-air services in the shopping mall? Is the vicar a football referee? Find points of contact with local readers/listeners.

6. Now phone the contact editors or producers and offer them your story. Ask if they would like a press release / interview / photo opportunity. Would they like your news regularly?

7. If appropriate, follow the phone call with a press release. This is a one-page summary of the story you are offering. Make it short and to the point. Include all details about time, date, venue and the event you want to promote. Try to find an interesting angle and provide a name and phone number for further information. (Make sure this person is easily available.) Use quotes to make the press release interesting.

8. If your story gets covered, and if it seems appropriate, follow through with a phone call to say thank you afterwards.

You can get more information about newspapers and magazines from *Willings Press Guide* (available in your local library), and about local radio from your local station or from *The Radio Authority Pocket Book*, available from The Radio Authority, Holbrook House, 14 Great Queen Street, London WC2B 5DG (tel: 0171 430 2724 fax: 0171 405 7062).

➤ # *SCHOOL ASSEMBLIES*

Many churches enjoy the privilege of access to a local school. The following ideas are aimed mainly at primary schools, but most of them can be adapted for use with older children. Whatever your level of experience of talking to school-age children, it's worth scanning the following advice before starting:

The four Vs

- *Be valid:* don't dilute the message; bring the whole truth. Remember your privileged position as the school's guest: your opportunity is educational rather than evangelistic.
- *Be visual:* have things to show or well-drawn acetates to use on an OHP.
- *Be vocal:* use music, even on a tape.
- *Be versatile:* know your audience (inner-city, suburban, rural) and tailor your style to them.

The Christmas present

Be visual. You will need a large box wrapped with bright Christmas paper and decorated to look as elaborate as possible. It should have a large label addressed to you. Inside should be a very dull, but useful, small present: e.g. a comb, a key-ring, a pair of socks.

Begin by talking about Christmas presents. Ask the children

about what they hope to get. Ask if they prefer big presents to small ones. (They probably will.) Invite a helper to the front. Build up the excitement about how exciting it is to receive a big present, and then bring out the large box. Make comments about its size, attractiveness and potential for containing something very special. What can be in it? Who is it for? Ask the child to read the label and open it for you. Close your eyes and wait. When the present is in your hands pretend to be very disappointed; look in the box to find the rest of it. Perhaps there's a cheque to go with it.

Talk about the present and the fact that, although it's small, it is really useful and is, in fact, just what you *needed* – but, of course, not quite what you *wanted*!

Tell the story of Jesus' birth. Emphasize the 'smallness' of the baby and point out that most of what we tend to see at Christmas-time is the story's 'wrapping': attractive but not essential. But the 'present' at the heart of Christmas is God's Son: the best, most useful gift we could ever have had.

Be vocal. All sing a carol or arrange for a small group of children to have prepared a song.

Be versatile. Talk about the fact that although, at the time, this birth was unnoticed, we still celebrate it today because Jesus is special – the best present we could have. With secondary school pupils, use the same format, but discuss the problem of embarrassing or unwanted Christmas presents. Do any of them turn out to be any good in the end?

The shepherd

Be visual. Dress as a shepherd; carry a fluffy toy lamb or sheep.

Tell the Christmas story from the point of view of one of the shepherds. Talk about the visit from the angels, their message of the birth and their invitation to visit the baby. Show the lamb and talk about taking the only thing you have to give as a present. ('I hope he'll like it!')

Tell the story as if you are on your way home, having seen the baby. Try to convey how this has affected you. The key to this style of presentation is to convey a sense of wonder at the 'specialness' of Jesus, of just how 'basic' the place of his birth was and how amazing it is that God's Son should be born in such poor surroundings. Finish the monologue by wondering what this baby might do when he grows up.

Be versatile. You can easily substitute the character of a wise man and talk about your gift, and about the star. An alternative approach could involve a final section in which you come out of character. Tell the children that your character was one of only a handful of people who knew about the birth of Jesus – and yet today, 2,000 years on, we are still talking about it.

For a secondary assembly, talk about the puzzling question: if this was God's Son, why was he born into such poverty? Coming out of character you could emphasize the way in which Jesus identifies with the world's poor and homeless because of the way in which he chose to come to us.

Leave a gift!

You will need to buy a copy of *The Fox's Story* by Nick Butterworth and Mick Inkpen (published by Harper Collins).

This retelling of the nativity story is particularly suited to children aged from five to seven. It features a fox who witnesses the appearance of the angels to the shepherds. He follows them and, more particularly, one of their lambs, to the place of Jesus' birth. Show the pictures as you tell the story. Here's a radical idea: at the end of assembly present the book to the school as a Christmas gift from your church.

The cracker

Be visual. Make or buy a large cracker containing a paper hat, a toy and a joke.

What do you have at a traditional Christmas lunch? Elicit suggestions from the children: turkey, Christmas pudding, candles... If nobody else has done so, suggest crackers and produce the one you have brought with you. Ask for suggestions about what might be inside. Invite two children to pull the cracker. Examine the toy, put on the hat and read the joke.

Tell the children that the cracker reminds you of the Christmas story.

Hold up the **toy**. Talk about God's gift to the world and explain about God sending Jesus. Put on the **hat**. Talk about Jesus being a king. Explain that he gave up his kingly status to come down to earth. Talk about how the world sees this as a **joke** and laughs at a story about a stable, shepherds and wise men.

Be versatile. For secondary assemblies major on the joke aspect. Discuss the amazing fact that we are still celebrating this festival at all. Also why not take the opportunity to dispel some of the 'false' elements which have been put into the story? (We don't know if Jesus was born on 25 December; it is unlikely to have been snowing; his visitors didn't all arrive on the same night – and so on.)

STIR-UP SUNDAY

➤ *AN ALL-AGE TALK FOR THE FIFTH SUNDAY BEFORE CHRISTMAS*

In the heyday of the *Book of Common Prayer* the 'Sunday next before Advent' was an exciting day in many homes, for people of all ages. It was the day to make Christmas puddings. This was due to the words of the collect for the day:

Stir up, we beseech thee, O Lord, the wills of thy faithful people; that they, plenteously bringing forth the fruit of good works, may of thee be plenteously rewarded; through Jesus Christ our Lord. Amen.

We still need to ask God to stir up our wills to yield fruit for him in his kingdom.

Here are some ideas for an all-age talk for Stir-up Sunday. It involves dialogue between the speaker and the congregation: the suggested responses from the congregation are shown in italics, within brackets. Make the questions your own, and be flexible if the answers aren't quite what you expect! It is based on 1 Peter. You will need equipment and ingredients for making a Christmas pudding.

A tasty chance

Does anybody know what this Sunday is called? *(Stir-up Sunday.)* What do we stir up today? *(A Christmas pudding.)* What does God want to stir up today? *(Us – our hearts!)* And what will be the result of this? *(We will want to love God more, and serve him better.)*

The collect asks God to stir us up. Do you think the church needs stirring up? Do you think we (the church) need stirring up? Let's make a Christmas pudding for the church. (Ask for a list of possible ingredients.) Which ingredient are you most like? God mixed different people together, for example: Jesus chose twelve apostles. Simon was possibly a zealot (a freedom fighter). Matthew was a tax collector (a collaborator). A recipe for conflict? Without Jesus they would have been at each other's throats. If they kept their eye on him they would work as a team. So, different as we are, we are mixed together in the church, God's faithful people. We all have separate wills. But they should combine for the good of each, for the good of all, for the glory of God and for the sake of the world.

God has a plan for us all in his church (1 Peter 1:4-5). We don't all wear dog-collars, but we are all holy. We might not like each part of the pudding, but the whole pudding is delightful to God. The pudding, the church, speaks of God to the world (1 Peter 2:9,10,12). Our wills need to be stirred up: to respond to God; to react properly with other people at church; to bring about change in our family, our community, our nation and in God's world.

What is *your* will with regard to God? To love him? To stand for him? To work and speak for him? To give your life for him?

(Start making your pudding at this point. Describe the contents as volunteers stir the mixture.)

Mix the dried fruit – the fruit of good works.

Flour – the cement of love.

Spices – special acts that give warmth.

Sugar – energy and vigour.

Breadcrumbs – ordinary actions.

Rind – difficult moments.

Suet – love to bind the mixture together.

Eggs – symbols of new life.

Brandy (or orange juice) – to keep the mixture moist.

The mixture should stand overnight – things don't happen all at once. It takes time for God to bind us together. It will need between four and eight hours' cooking – it takes time for God to make us what he wants us to be. It takes time, heat and often pressure (as in a pressure cooker). The ingredients are actually changed during the cooking. Can you imagine changing for God? Can you imagine the church changing for God?

Stir up, O Lord, the wills of your faithful people.

God can change us into the likeness of Jesus. How should we behave while the changing takes place (1 Peter 3:8-9)? You can't cook with ingredients that refuse to mix! There is a blessing on offer – what is it (1 Peter 3:10-12)? *(Happiness.)* There are also some conditions: what are they? *(Guard your tongue. Turn from evil and do good. Strive for peace.)* God sees the righteous and hears their prayers.

Activity

At the end of the teaching message invite the whole congregation to stir the pudding mixture as a symbol of their willingness to be stirred up and changed by God. (They should be encouraged to say a prayer, rather than make a wish!)

Follow-up

At an all-age service on Christmas Day the pudding can be served (re-heated in a microwave) with a small portion of cream as a celebration of the 'body life' of the church.

Stir up, O Lord, the wills of your faithful people; that richly bearing the fruit of good works, they may by you be richly rewarded; through Jesus Christ our Lord. Amen. (ASB)

A TALK FOR ADULTS

➤ *TRUTH OR TRADITION?*

Western society and theology traditionally paint a very bleak picture of the situation of Mary and Joseph on their arrival in Bethlehem that first Christmas. We think of a wintry, wind-blown town and of the futile attempt of the couple to find accommodation. The reality may well have been very different.

The birth of Jesus – an alternative view

The weather. The tradition of celebrating Christmas on 25 December goes back to the time when the church chose to 'christianize' the old pagan midwinter festival. Luke's narrative does not suggest 'bleak midwinter'. It certainly could not have been too cold at the time because the sheep were out at night (Luke 2:8). In really cold weather the sheep would have been kept indoors at night and grazed out in the day.

The family. When Joseph and his pregnant wife travelled to Bethlehem they were going to his ancestral home. From the Gospels we know that they had a network of relatives in the Bethlehem area. For example, Zechariah and Elizabeth lived near Jerusalem, only a short distance from Bethlehem. In Eastern society, then as now, the family is made up of an extended group of people with a patriarch at the head. Married children and their children live with or near the father and mother. The authority and protection of the father extends to them and their respect and obedience is expected in return. Relatives from other towns are welcomed by the patriarch and brought under his protection during their stay in his village.

The house. The architecture of the family home, both now and in antiquity, made provision for the occasional guest. The traditional house had several levels. The lower room, or cellar, was used as a storeroom and stable for the animals. Here they were fed and sheltered, protected from the cold and from thieves. This was often a cave which was incorporated into the house when it was built. The main living area, upstairs, was a large living room / kitchen. In this room food was prepared and eaten and at night it became a bedroom for the children. There was also a separate bedroom for the parents and, in wealthier houses, a guest room. The Greek word *kataluma* (usually translated as 'inn'), can also be translated as 'guest room'. Is it possible that it was here, rather than in an inn, that Mary and Joseph were unable to find accommodation?

Home or away? Returning to his paternal home for the census, it's likely that Joseph followed Middle-Eastern custom and went straight to the family home for help and protection. However, the family guest room was already full and there was no private place where Mary could have her baby, that is until someone thought of the cellar / stable. Mary could go downstairs and have the baby in the warmth of the cellar / stable while attended by women relatives from upstairs. Joseph would have the company of his male relatives as he waited for the delivery. Both Mary and Joseph may well have been safe within the security of a family for the birth – not abandoned and isolated as Western tradition suggests. The traditional site of the cellar / stable is in the centre of the city where family homes would have stood rather than in the surrounding countryside.

If this is what happened on that first Christmas night it puts a new light on our Christmas celebrations. Mary and Joseph may not have been the outcasts we assume them to have been. Instead they were squeezed in among kinsfolk and no doubt it was a grand family occasion made more special by the birth of a baby – a joyful night in spite of the soldiers outside.

So perhaps our Christmas celebration where all the family gathers for a feast is not as far removed from that first Christmas as we have sometimes been led to believe.

Cut-away view of a Palestinian house

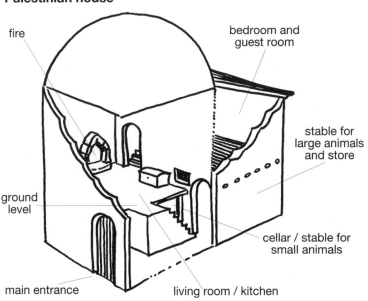

fire

bedroom and guest room

stable for large animals and store

ground level

cellar / stable for small animals

main entrance

living room / kitchen

The house had small windows and no chimney.

Another Palestinian house

In this house too we see the two-level construction with one common entrance. The upper floor is the living accommodation whilst the lower shelters the animals and gives storage space. The lower floor is built into the hillside and may even be built over a cave.

CELEBRATING WITH YOUNG CHILDREN

➤ *EVENTS*

Holiday clubs

Why do we stick to summer-time holiday clubs? The Christmas story has the whole gospel contained in it and you won't have a shortage of children to hear it. Most parents will appreciate the opportunity to have their children safely occupied while they complete their shopping.

Parties

Celebrate the real reason for the season with the children from your group. A party is an ideal opportunity for them to be the evangelists as they invite their friends.

Serving the community

How about encouraging the children in your groups to 'put something on' for other members of the community, whether young or old? Perform a nativity in an old folks' home; hold a Christmas Fair with the children making cakes, craft items or 'busking' (send money raised to a Christmas charity such as Christmas Cracker or Crisis at Christmas); go carol singing to raise money (have you got a children's hospital near you that you could go to?).

➤ *WORSHIP AND TALK IDEAS*

Christingle

The gospel message contained in an orange, a candle, some cocktail sticks, a red ribbon and some sweets! This is a relatively new service that gives the reason for Christmas with an individual visual aid. Originally designed to raise money for the Children's Society, it revolves around Jesus being the light of the world (the candle in the orange) and with his blood shed for all (the red ribbon around the orange). Details from The Children's Society, Edward Rudolph House, 69 Margery Street, London WC1X 0LJ (tel: 0171 837 4299).

Immanuel – God is with us

Take time to think what this name actually means – God on earth, with us, to save us. Look at the other Old Testament names of Jesus from Isaiah 9, Micah 5. Emphasize that God had been preparing for the big event of the birth of his Son for many years: make a link with our anticipation and excitement for Christmas. Are we ever disappointed? Were the people of Israel disappointed with who Jesus was?

Pass the parcel

Play 'pass the parcel' (in church or with your children's group) and under each layer of paper have something associated with secular Christmas (the *Radio Times*, a party popper, tinsel, etc.). In the middle have something to represent Jesus. Talk about what Christmas is really all about.

Video interviews

If you can borrow a camcorder, go to your High Street and ask people to say what they think Christmas means. Watch the video and discuss their answers. Ask if this is what God intended for Christmas. Perhaps older children could conduct the interviews themselves.

➤ *CRAFT*

Angels

Essential to any Christmas craft! Follow the illustration.

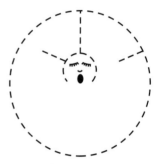

Mobiles

Make up a number of basic shapes and string them up to a coat hanger or, if you're feeling adventurous, to balanced wood kebab skewers (see illustration). Use stars with glitter, sheep and shepherds with plenty of cotton wool, little boxes wrapped up with a bow on, little socks (cut-out cardboard or material), angels (mini versions of the above), holly leaves and so on.

Potato printing

Make Christmas cards using potato prints. Use a basic triangle printer to make patterns that look like a Christmas tree. Decorate with stuck-on glitter and sticky stars.

Banners

Make a large banner of the Christmas story to present to the church. If you can't draw, photocopy or trace simple outline pictures of the story characters (try looking in a colouring book) and provide material for the children to fill in the pictures as templates. Choose a suitable verse and make the letters by gluing paper letters face down on to the wrong side of material. When they're dry, cut around the outline so the material doesn't fray.

Cooking

Get some festive pastry cutters and make biscuits in Christmas shapes. You could also use the pastry cutters to cut out modelling material (such as 'Fimo'), put a hole in the top, bake them and thread a string through to make decorations.

➤ *THE JESSE TREE*

The Jesse Tree was a popular image in medieval Christian art. It represented the ancestry of Jesus in the form of a tree rising from the sleeping body of David's father, Jesse. Organize a children's craft morning (or day) a couple of weeks before Christmas to prepare a 'Jesse Tree' as an alternative to the customary Christmas tree with its traditional decorations.

Prepare a large tree outline. Use the following symbols (or others of your own choice). Arrange them in chronological order with creation close to the tree's stem and the symbols for Jesus close to the top.

Pentecost

Resurrection

Salvation

Feeding of 5,000

Light of the world

The Annunciation

Daniel

Exile

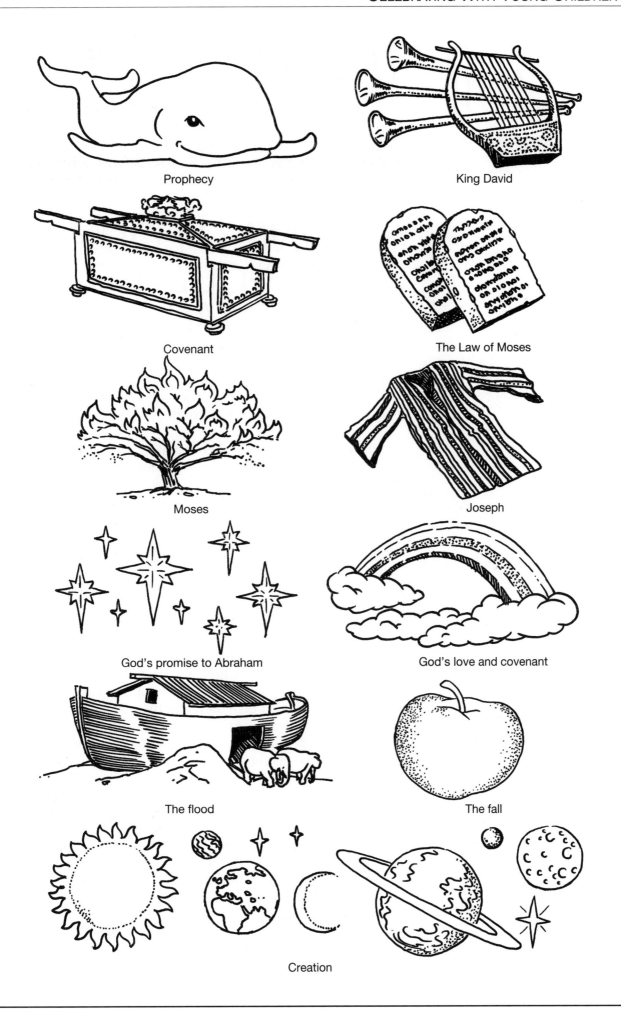

Prophecy

King David

Covenant

The Law of Moses

Moses

Joseph

God's promise to Abraham

God's love and covenant

The flood

The fall

Creation

BUILDING BRIDGES

► *PLANNING FOR A CROSS-CULTURAL CHRISTMAS*

Ida Glaser, Other Faiths Secretary of Crosslinks, outlines simple ways in which a church can share the joy and excitement of Christmas with people from a variety of cultural backgrounds and from differing faith communities.

It's **Diwali**, and the Hindus are celebrating. They go to the temple, light lamps to celebrate the victory of light over darkness, and tell the stories of Lakhshmi who visits lighted houses with gifts of prosperity, and of Vishnu's preservation of the world through the defeat of the demon Bali. Then they prepare a wonderful spread and open their doors, and *everyone* comes to visit – family, friends and all the neighbours, Muslim, agnostic, Buddhist and Christian.

It's **'Id ul-Fitr**, and the Muslims are celebrating. They put on new clothes, and go to the mosque to thank God for helping them to fast through Ramadan. They prepare a wonderful spread and they open their doors, and *everyone* comes to visit – family, friends and all the neighbours, Buddhist, Hindu, agnostic and Christian.

It's **Christmas**, and the Christians are celebrating. They go to church to celebrate the birth of Jesus Christ. Then they prepare a wonderful spread. And then they shut themselves up in their houses with their families, stuff themselves and watch television? No! They open their doors, and *everyone* comes to visit – family, friends and all the neighbours, Buddhist, Muslim, agnostic, Hindu, anyone and everyone who lives nearby and wants to wish them well and to share their celebration.

At least, that's how it happens in Malaysia, where I had the privilege of living for two years, and in many other Christian communities around the world.

Christmas – opportunity knocks

Festivals celebrated by people of different faiths are times of hospitality: they are opportunities to visit, to get to know people and to have fun together. Christian festivals can also be times of hospitality: there is no reason why British Christians shouldn't copy their overseas brothers and sisters and take more of a lead in opening their homes and communities at festival times. And what better time than Christmas to start to break down some of the barriers of mistrust that so divide our society and hamper our mission?

Most people know the outline of the Christmas story, as it is usually covered at school. Muslims, in particular, are able to participate in Christmas. They deny the death of Jesus, but the Qur'an tells the story of his birth in terms very similar to Luke's Gospel.

Muslims feel at ease with Christmas – but they do not know the true identity of the child born in the stable. They know Jesus as a prophet, but their strong monotheism makes the idea of God having a son unthinkable. Christmas is a time to begin to explain what we mean by 'Son of God' – that God has come to us, that his Word has become flesh, as a person, not simply as a book, the Qur'an.

Parties

Geoff and Jane took over the local church hall. They already knew lots of Asian children, and some had played games in the hall before. So it was not a strange place to them. Word went round that there was going to be a Christmas party. Mums were invited to make food. Several energetic helpers from the church were enlisted. Prizes were bought, and games and stories planned. It was an exhausting day, but about fifty children, mostly Muslims, enjoyed games and quizzes, and heard about the coming of Jesus.

Or how about an International Party? In an area that is very mixed culturally, people can be invited to bring food or to present an item from their own background, and a Christian drama can be included.

Carol singing

In many countries, people have street processions to celebrate festivals. It seems natural to them that Christians should sing praises to God in the streets at Christmas. Often, Muslim or Hindu children will come out and join in.

Christmas Day

Dinner can be difficult, as people from different faiths have different food regulations. *Halal* turkeys – that can be eaten by Muslims – are available from most Muslim butchers, and of course you can't have bacon or sausage meat stuffing. *Halal* turkeys tend to be much tastier than the supermarket variety. For Hindus and Sikhs, you may have to offer a vegetarian alternative. Remember that suet (in mince pies and Christmas puddings) is an animal derivative, and that any form of alcohol may be prohibited to your Asian friends.

Following dinner, I have an 'open house', to which neighbours of different faiths are welcome. I bake cakes and biscuits, and, if any are left over, I remember that most of my neighbours have the tradition of taking celebration food to neighbours. That gives me the opportunity to visit people who have not visited me.

I also have a Christmas tree hung with inexpensive presents: books about Christmas, coloured pencils, small toys. Every child may choose a gift. Under the tree are calendars with Bible verses in English and appropriate Asian languages, as well as copies of Luke's Gospel for anyone who wants to learn more of the Christmas story.

Chrismas Day can be very chaotic, but I think of the people who come to my home as my birthday gift to Jesus.

Services

Christmas can also be a good time to invite people to church. Many will have learned carols at school, and will enjoy a carol service. Some are eager to see how we celebrate!

● An Asian Christian fellowship makes a point of inviting non-Christian friends to Christmas and Easter services. Some Muslims have been happy to come, and some have been attracted to Christ.

● We ensure that part of the Christmas leaflet that is distributed to every home in the parish is in a relevant Asian language, and invite people especially to our carol service. We make sure that some of the after-service mince pies are vegetarian, and we have people from different cultures contributing to the service. We also educate church members in how to behave appropriately to Asian people of the opposite sex.

Christmas comes but once a year...

... and there are 364 other days. The sort of Christmas I have described can launch us into better relationships for the next year, but it's difficult to make it effective if there have been no relationships in the preceding year. People will be happier to visit us if we have already visited them – perhaps at their festivals. You can visit a neighbour without an invitation, especially during a celebration. This is part of the joy of many cultures. May we share that joy as we share with others the Joy that has come into the world.

For further help

Celebration of Faith. This booklet comes from the Other Faiths Coalition of the Evangelical Alliance. It aims to help Christians to understand the festivals of a variety of faiths and to think about their responses to them, especially in schools. It is available from The Evangelical Alliance, Whitefield House, 186 Kennington Park Road, London SE11 4BT.

CPAS / Crosslinks Other Faiths Consultancy is a service that puts local churches in touch with resources and people who can help them move forward in their mission to people of other faiths. Contact Mark Smith at CPAS or Ida Glaser at CROSSLINKS, 251 Lewisham Way, London SE4 1XF.

South Asian Concern offers help with alternative Diwali celebrations: PO Box 43, Sutton, Surrey SM2 5WL.

A SEEKER-FRIENDLY CHRISTMAS

➤ SEEKER-FRIENDLY EVENTS

Many people make their one-and-only visit to a church at Christmas. For an increasing number of our 'unchurched' friends, neighbours and workmates, to enter a church building or to go to a church-sponsored event is to venture into alien territory. The words they hear, the sights they see and the whole 'culture' in which they find themselves participating is strange and unfamiliar.

Being 'seeker-friendly' is all about being sensitive to the many barriers that separate us, the 'churched' people, from men and women with little or no experience of what goes on in the average service. Even the most informal church event can seem threatening and excluding unless everyone involved makes a conscious effort to try and communicate across the culture gap.

When planning any Christmas event to which first-time visitors are invited, use the following check-list to help increase its level of seeker-friendliness.

1. Try holding your event at a venue that's different from your regular choice of meeting place – a sports hall, hotel conference room, restaurant, village hall, night club. Combine it with a social activity.
2. Produce an attractive, eye-catching programme card for the event and hand one to each visitor as they arrive.
3. Christmas is a time for giving. Why not give a small, inexpensive gift to everyone as part of the service / event? Most unchurched people are impressed when the church gives rather than takes.
4. Think about the seating layout for the event. What about in the round, a semi-circle or in small groups?
5. Invite a local school to participate. Give the music teacher two or three contemporary Christmas songs for the children to perform. You may double your numbers when the parents come to see their children.
6. Divide the 'talk' into two or three 'bite-sized' chunks using

lots of real-life stories and visual aids.

7. Use the Bible creatively with readings in a variety of styles: dramatically with two or more readers; using background music; miming the passage to accompany a dramatic reading; 'performing' the passage from memory.

8. Use coloured acetates for the OHP, and some Christmas clip-art graphics.

9. Why not include an interview, drama, children's dance to a carol or song, poetry or slide or video sequence set to music?

10. Invite your local MP, mayor, councillor – not for an official visit, but simply to support what you are doing.

11. Serve a well-presented supper before or after the event.

12. Invest in some good quality publicity to be used as personal invitations. Give the event an attractive, non-churchy title.

13. Produce a simple outline of the talk for people to take away, suggesting things they can think through and some practical steps they can take.

➤ *THREE SEEKER-FRIENDLY SKETCHES*

The meaning of Christmas

This sketch explores the relevance of many Christmas traditions to the real purpose of the celebration.

Cast: *Mum and Daughter, both busily preparing for the arrival of family for Christmas Day.*

Daughter:	When's my birthday, Mum?
Mum:	The fourteenth of July. Why?
Daughter:	Well, it's Jesus' birthday today, isn't it? I wish I could have my birthday on Christmas Day.
Mum:	Your Dad and I have enough to do at Christmas, without having your birthday to cope with as well.
Daughter:	Jesus' Dad seems to manage OK.
Mum:	Well, he's had more experience of organizing things. Now be a good girl and hold the other end of this streamer.
Daughter:	Mum, did Mary and Joseph decorate the stable?
Mum:	I shouldn't think so. They didn't have streamers when Jesus was born. Now, pass me the tape and we'll finish wrapping Dad's present.
Daughter:	The wise men brought presents for Jesus, didn't they?
Mum:	Yes, they did.
Daughter:	Do you think he got lots of socks like Dad?
Mum:	No, dear. Jesus was only a tiny baby – just like you were.
Daughter:	*(Pause)* Just like me? Exactly like me?
Mum:	Yes – just like you were.
Daughter:	*(Disappointed)* Oh.
Mum:	Right, pop this present under the tree and we'll put

the rest of the baubles on the tree.

Daughter: *(Pause)* Mum... did Mary and Joseph decorate a Christmas tree for baby Jesus?

Mum: I don't think so, dear. I don't think they had much time for that sort of thing. No disposable nappies in those days... down to the river with your dirty swaddling clothes... yuk. Now, you finish that while I put these cards up.

Daughter: Did the shepherds and wise men send Jesus cards? Did he have millions and millions of cards?

Mum: *(Impatiently)* No, dear, cards were invented by the Victorians... I think. In Jesus' day they would just have had to go and see him. *(Pause)* Hmm, doesn't that look Christmassy. Now... we'll just set the table and then we'll be ready for Grandad and Granny, won't we?

Daughter: I bet they had a huge party for Jesus, didn't they? I expect everybody wanted to come.

Mum: Well, no, they didn't. King Herod wanted to have baby Jesus killed and they had to go away and hide in another country.

Daughter: *(Long pause)* Mum... if Jesus didn't have all these things when he was born, why do we have them?

Covert operations

Theme: God's plan of salvation

Scene: *The sketch is set in heaven a few hours before the birth of Jesus.*

Cast: *Archangel Michael (Captain of the Heavenly Host); Tal, another angel.*

Tal is pacing up and down. Michael stares into the distance.

Michael: Peace be with you.

Tal: Sir!

Michael: It's Tal, isn't it?

Tal: Yes, sir... Er?

Michael: I'm Michael – the Archangel, Michael.

Tal: Yes, sir! Er...

Michael: Yes?

Tal: What brings you to heaven's gate tonight, sir?

Michael: I wanted to take a closer look at the Earth before the operation begins. You look uneasy. What's the matter, Tal?

Tal: Sorry, sir. It's just that there are only a few hours to go, and it's not going as I expected.

Michael: What did you expect? This is the biggest covert operation heaven has ever mounted.

Tal: Yes, but... He's going himself this time. Is that safe?

Michael: Safe? Not at all. Focusing all the divine presence into one human life – of course it isn't safe! But he knows what he's doing.

Tal: Is everything ready?

Michael: It will be. The family is in Bethlehem; and we have accommodation planned for the mother and child *(with a hint of wry humour)*. We have the star ready to become a supernova, and Gabriel is going to accompany the heavenly host.

Tal: Yes, but that's exactly what puzzles me. The Son is going to take on an ordinary human life. We've kept security tight until now. So why risk this extravagant display of glory to men on the hillsides around Bethlehem? The enemy can't fail to see it!

Michael: We shall be there in sufficient force to ward off any approach.

Tal: I think you've missed my point, sir. What about afterwards? Aren't we exposing him to attack right through his childhood – we're breaking his cover too soon!

Michael: We know the enemy's intelligence is not perfect, Tal, but we can't conceal the whereabouts of Jesus for long. That's not the point of the plan.

Tal: I thought that he would need time... time to grow to understand what it means to be a man. If the enemy wakes up to what is happening, the whole world of evil is going to come down on him. And what then?

Michael: He's going to have to face that. This plan isn't designed to avoid confrontation with evil. What matters is how he reveals himself to ordinary men and women.

Tal: What do you mean?

Michael: Well, a magnificent arrival and a public display of force would not achieve the right result. Men and women of goodwill will find him soon enough, and they'll recognize him for who he is. This way they'll follow for love – and not for glory!

Tal: I know the power of love. And I know he's deliberately taking a risk of rejection. But won't he need to take reasonable force – enough to stop the enemy from moving in to take his life?

Michael: All the heavenly host will be ready at his command – but somehow I don't think we're going to be needed (pause). We've yet to see the lengths to which love will go!

Lads

Theme: Why celebrate?

Props: A table, two chairs, one newspaper, one magazine, two pint glasses of brown liquid and a handkerchief.

Cast: Phil, Steve

(Phil sits reading paper. Steve arrives with drinks. They begin drinking and carry on reading)

Phil: You goin' to go to church this Christmas, then?

Steve: No, goin' to the wife's mother's. (Phil groans) How about you – you goin' to church then?

Phil: Well, this year we thought we'd 'ave a real traditional Christmas.

Steve: What you mean – peace on earth an' good will towards men an' all that sort of stuff?

Phil: No. I just mean that I think it's important to think about others at Christmas time.

Steve: (Sarcastically) An' goin' to church will 'elp, will it?

Phil: Look (moving closer), the incarnation is very important.

Steve: I prefer custard myself.

Phil: (Slowly) The in-car-nation.

Steve: What, you mean coming back as a cow or summat?

Phil: (Loudly) The incarnation!

Steve:	Well, wha's that then?
Phil:	The incarnation, see, is where God's Son comes down to earth an' is born to the virgin Mary in a stable, because there is no room in the pub.
Steve:	Well there wouldn't be, would there?
Phil:	What?
Steve:	There wouldn't be any room in the pub. They're always full at Christmas.
Phil:	See, that's the trouble with you, you don't think enough. See, there wasn't any Christmas before Jesus was born. That's what we're supposed to celebrate.
Steve:	What, no presents?
Phil:	Na.
Steve:	No Christmas dinner?
Phil:	Na.
	(Dialogue gradually speeds up)
Steve:	Carols?
Phil:	Na.
Steve:	Christmas trees?
Phil:	Na.
Steve:	Crackers?
Phil:	Na.
Steve:	Holly?
Phil:	Na.
Steve:	Decorations?
Phil:	Na.
Steve:	No ding donging merrily on high with Little Red Riding Goose and the Babes up the Beanstalk?
Phil:	Na. And there were no pantomimes neither. It all started with a baby in a manger. That's why people celebrated; to thank God for the gift of Jesus.
Steve:	Yeah, but you don' believe that rubbish, do you?
Phil:	I don't know. It's gotta be worth thinking about. If it is true it must be one of the most amazing things that's ever happened, you see...
Steve:	*(Interrupting)* Cliff Richard!
Phil:	You wha'?
Steve:	Cliff Richard; 'e's one a them Christians, in't 'e?
Phil:	Well I suppose...
Steve:	*(Interrupting)* Terry Wogan?
Phil:	Is he a Christian? I never knew that.
Steve:	Yeah. He spent five years in captivity as an 'ostage.
Phil:	That's not Terry Wogan, that's Terry Waite.
Steve:	Shoulda bin Terry Wogan.
Phil:	Yeah.
Steve:	Mind you, I bet half of the people what go to them churches at Christmas don't believe it.
Phil:	Why do you say that?
Steve:	Well they only go once a year, don't they?
Phil:	You mean they're hypocrites?
Steve:	I don't think their star sign has anything to do with it; I just reckon they don't believe it. If you go at all you ought to go regular. *(Pause)* Anyway, I don't believe it. If I was God I would

not let any son of mine get born in a stable. If it was true then this God's as daft as a brush. All the posh hotels he could have chosen an' 'e goes an' lets his son get born at the back of the Bethlehem Rose and Crown. It don't seem in keeping wiv 'is nature.

Phil: That's the point. See (*moving in closer as if telling a secret*), if he had come in might and majesty flying on a cloud he would have been forcing people to believe in 'im. By being born in a stable nobody could accuse him of cheating. He was just an ordinary guy goin' round doin' good and tellin' people to be nice to each other.

Steve: So they crucified 'im?

Phil: Yeah. Well no, they didn't crucify 'im for that. They crucified him for pretending to be God.

Steve: But you just said 'e was God?

Phil: Yeah, no, I mean yeah, 'e was God; but they didn't know that.

Steve: They didn't think 'e was, so they crucified 'im for pretending to be. It gets a bit complicated, don't it? So you reckon going to church once a year will make it all right between you an' God?

Phil: Well, I...

Steve: (*Doesn't let him finish*) Will it make up for what you did with that Maureen while your missus was away?

Phil: I think...

Steve: (*Interrupts again*) Let me tell you, mate (*laughing*), it'll take more than a morning in church to repent for that one, I should say.

Phil: That's not the point.

Steve: What is the point then?

Phil: See, look here, God like understands us. He sees into the secrets of our hearts and he knows that I'm not ignoring him just because I don't go to church every week. God can see into your heart.

Steve: What can he see?

Phil: In your case about three crates of brown ale an' a lot of chips.

Steve: So what you doin' after church then?

Phil: Down the pub, few beers, back home, kick the kids, pig out on Christmas lunch, then fall asleep in front of the Queen on the telly until it's time to open a few cans of ale.

Steve: Glad to see you aren't letting this religious stuff go to your head then.

Phil: Na. (*Raising glass*) Cheers.

Steve: (*Responding*) Merry Christmas, mate, merry Christmas. (*To audience*) And to you lot, merry Christmas to you too.

FAMILY SERVICE TALKS

➤ *GIFT RAP!*

The following talks for family services take their theme from John 3:16.

A piece of straw

This talk was inspired by seeing a pile of straw beneath a church's decorated Christmas tree. The speaker goes to the tree, picks up a handful of straw and says:

I would like to give you all a Christmas present to tie on your tree at home. But first, have you been helping with the Christmas tree decorations this year? What have you put on the tree? Any really old decorations which were used by grandparents? Any new ones this year? Any lights?

What do you put at the top of the tree? A star? An angel? Either one reminds us of the birth of Jesus.

Did anyone put a piece of straw on the tree? I like to put a piece of straw on our tree at home. Looks pretty useless on its own, a single piece of straw.

When Jesus was born the Roman army and government controlled Palestine. For many years, nearly four hundred in fact, the Romans also controlled Britain. During all that time they had a phrase for worthless things. They used to say, 'Well, that's not worth a straw.'

But if you think about it, straw is actually very useful. We use it to make beds for animals and, in some parts of the world, for people. We use it to thatch roofs on houses in lots of places here and abroad. It's also often used in making clay bricks. We use it to protect crops and vegetables from frost and ground damage. We use it for packing things safely. (*Invite people to suggest further uses for straw.*)

But why put a piece of straw on your Christmas tree? If you look carefully you will see a piece of straw on the tree here in church. It's a reminder about Jesus. He was born in a stable; I think there would have been quite a lot of straw around there. And at the end of his life he was treated by the Romans, and others, as being worthless – not worth a straw.

Perhaps it could also be a gentle warning to us not to treat

Jesus as worthless. We can know Jesus as being worth far more than we could ever understand. Surely the best gift we could ever have at Christmas is to know him as a true friend. His good news lasts for ever, even when the sky and the earth have gone.

You see, God has a habit of taking what *seems* worthless and making something better out of it – a bit like the way he treats you and me!

So if I give each of you a piece of straw, please take it home and put it on your tree amidst the other decorations and then when people say, 'What's that bit of useless straw doing on your tree?' you can say, 'Oh, that's to remind me of my king and friend, Jesus.'

Unwrapping God's present

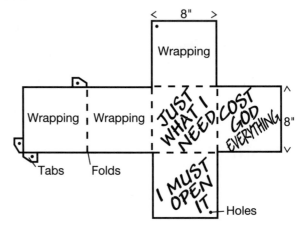

Prepare a box in the form of a cube. You will need six 20cm squares of card connected together in such a way that when opened up they form a cross shape. Line the 'inside' with brightly coloured paper.

Write one of the following statements on the inside faces of the cube:

New Life by Jesus' Death

What a Gift!

The connected squares should now be folded and, with careful pinning, a box can be produced.

The outside of the box should have three adjacent sides covered in Christmas wrapping paper. On the three other sides write the points you wish to make. Choose some of the following, or write your own:

FREE TO ME   **I MUST OPEN IT!**   **COST GOD EVERYTHING**

UNEXPECTED?   **JUST WHAT I NEED!**

Begin the talk by showing the box with its Christmas wrapping paper. Talk about Christmas gifts. Be careful not to let the congregation see the faces with writing on them.

Now rotate the box to reveal each face in turn. Finally unclip the box to find out what's inside. You then reveal the cross shape with the 'inner' message words written on it.

Don't miss out!

Prepare six wrapped presents as follows:

Present 1. A large box, attractively wrapped, but containing nothing. Attached is a large gift tag: 'For the person who has got everything, from Miss Erable.'

Emphasize the fact that you like opening big presents first. Express disappointment on finding nothing inside and make the connection with Miss Erable being really miserable.

Present 2. This present is also neatly wrapped with a gift tag, and is from Miss Fitt. Inside is a jumper which is either too small or too large. Show delight about getting a new jumper and then disappointment that it is no use because it does not fit. Miss Fitt definitely lives up to her name!

Present 3. Open to find a box of chocolates. Show delight and enthusiasm followed by disappointment on finding only one chocolate left in the box. There is a note saying, 'Sorry – I felt a little bit hungry when I was wrapping.' The gift tag is from Miss Greedy. Eat the chocolate quickly and emphasize the fact that this present was nice, but did not last very long.

Present 4. You are now hoping desperately that you will get a suitable present. Again disappointment! It contains a neatly wrapped pair of odd socks. The gift tag reads: 'From Miss Match.'

Present 5. Pretend that this is the last present to be opened and again express disappointment when you find out that it is no use. It should contain something that's inappropriate to the gender of the opener: after-shave for a woman or lipstick for a man. This time the gift tag is from Miss Take. Miss Take is really mistaken!

Talk about how much you were looking forward to opening these presents. They were all beautifully wrapped and looked very promising. Yet when you opened them some were no use, some were totally unsuitable and some did not last very long. What a disappointing Christmas.

Then find one last small present.
Present 6. This will consist of a large sheet of paper folded up into the smallest possible size and wrapped in brown paper. There is no gift tag. On one side of the sheet of paper is written, 'With love from God' and on the other, 'Jesus'.

Discuss whether you should open this present because it is so small and isn't as nicely wrapped as the others. Yet you wonder where it has come from.

Open the present and unfold the sheet of paper. Hold up the side which says 'With love from God'. This seems a very special gift because it is from God and it comes with love. What sort of gift could God give to us? Turn the paper round to show the word 'Jesus'.

Make the following points about God's gift:
1. God gave this gift because he knew what we really needed.

2. The gift of Jesus is for everyone, including you and me: 'For God so loved the world.'
3. This is a very precious gift which cost God so much – his only Son.
4. Other presents will wear out but the gift of Jesus is for ever. It gives us everlasting life.
5. Like all Christmas gifts, we need to receive and open the gift which God has given us. We receive the gift by believing (trusting) in Jesus and we open it by opening our lives and inviting him to be our friend.
6. Don't let us miss the most important gift this Christmas.

Present tense?

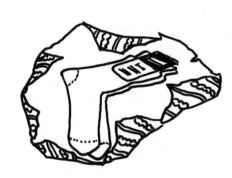

Fill a box or sack with wrapped Christmas presents in each of the following categories:

1. Unwanted present – for example, a record by a once-popular, but now cringe-worthy, pop star.
2. Misunderstood present – for example, a household gadget whose use you can seem to fail to understand.
3. Inappropriate present – for example, hair gel for a bald person.
4. Expected presents – something safe and predictable.
5. Unexpected present – ask someone else to prepare this present so that it is a genuine surprise.
6. Unimaginative present – something even more safe and predictable.
7. Unused present – a 're-cycled', unwanted gift from a previous Christmas.
8. Forgotten present – leave this one on one side, to be 'discovered' at the end of the talk.

Open all the presents except for the forgotten one. Give an exaggeratedly appropriate response to each one: surprise, boredom, etc. Copy the titles on to acetates and display on the OHP as you talk about each present.

Unwanted present. We have all had unwanted presents at Christmas, sometimes a joke (like this record), sometimes more serious. Illness, marital break-up and bereavement may all happen at Christmas time – the sort of Christmas presents nobody wants. For some the gift of Jesus at Christmas is an unwanted present – they just want to get on with their lives without any interference from God. He is an unwanted complication in their lives. 'I want to do what I want to do.'

Misunderstood present. For some, Christmas is a misunderstood present. In the time of Jesus some people thought he was coming as a freedom fighter, a revolutionary who would kick the Romans out of Palestine, a national hero who would make Israel great again. People still misunderstand why Jesus came. His life had a very special purpose that can only be understood if we know the Easter story as well as the Christmas story, about a God who loves us so much that he shares death as well as birth, about a God who wants to be friends with us so much that he dies in order that we might be forgiven and have a new start.

Inappropriate present. Hair gel for a bald man? Some people think of God's Christmas gift to us a bit like that. Jesus is all right, but we don't see how he fits into our life. People may say, 'My life is too much of a mess'; 'I'm not the religious type'; 'I'm OK as I am – I don't need that Jesus stuff.' But if God is creator and maker of us all, he designed the world and us, and if he thinks we need Jesus, then maybe there's something in it. And look at the Gospels: men and women from all backgrounds found purpose for their lives in Jesus.

Expected and unexpected presents. You know some presents are coming, others are a complete surprise. When Jesus was born some people were waiting for him. Some people today are like that. When they come to know Jesus, it's as if all along they knew there had to be something like this. They've been waiting to hear about it all their lives. But others find him the last thing they expect, they are surprised by the Christian gospel, they never expected anything like this, that someone could love them so much to give up everything for them.

Unimaginative present. God's gift of Jesus isn't like that. Who would have dreamed that if God wanted to come into the world he would be born in poverty? Who would have dreamed he would have come to the backwater of Galilee? Who would have dreamed that he would have made friends with society's outcasts? Who would have believed he would have been killed by a gruesome instrument of torture and then rise again and set about changing the world by sending out a handful of ordinary working people? Well, he did. God's certainly got imagination! And that's what it's like when you walk with God. You don't know what's coming next. It's certainly not a case of 'oh, no, socks again'.

Forgotten and unused presents. The saddest of all. Have you ever bought anyone an expensive or special present only to find that person has forgotten or lost your gift? It's heartbreaking, isn't it? Don't forget God's good gift of his Son to you this year.

A CAROL SERVICE

➤ *THE WOMEN OF GOD*

Each member of the congregation should have a service sheet with the order of the readings and the titles of the carols and choir items.

The opening readings of the Annunciation (Luke 1:26-38) and Mary's visit to Elizabeth (Luke 1:39-45) should be read by a younger woman and an older woman respectively.

As an alternative to a traditional reading of Hannah's story, use the version of 1 Samuel 1:1-20 in *The Dramatised Bible* (Marshall Pickering). For a powerful impact of the Magnificat text (Luke 1:46-55), choose a confident reader who is willing to memorize the passage.

For contrast, choose male readers for the passage from Isaiah 9 and for the story of the shepherds (Luke 2:8-20). For the narrative from Matthew 2, let a male reader take verses 1-12 and hand over to a woman to complete the passage (verses 16-18).

Introduction

Brothers and sisters in Christ, be it this Christmastide our duty and joy to hear again the message of the angels, and in heart and mind to go again to Bethlehem and see this thing which is come to pass, and the Babe, lying in the manger.

Therefore let us read and mark in Holy Scripture the loving purposes of God in history. Let us reflect on the faithful obedience of Mary; let us see the strength she draws from the miracle of birth in the life of her kinswoman Elizabeth. Let us hear of the holy women of God in the Old Testament who received the promise of God and believed it against the odds. And let us hear again the events of that most holy night as a Child is born, as shepherds wonder, as angels sing, as wise men pay homage and light is born into our world, a light which shines in the darkness and which the darkness cannot put out.

Carol:	Once in royal David's city
Reading:	Luke 1:26-38
Carol:	Child in a manger
Reading:	Luke 1:39-45
Choir:	Choral item
Readings:	Genesis 17:15-22
	To Sarah is promised the child Isaac, father of Israel
	1 Samuel 1:1-20
	To Hannah is promised the child Samuel, prophet of Israel
	Luke 1:46-55
	Mary in her obedience praises the God of promise
Carol:	O little town of Bethlehem
Readings:	Isaiah 9:2-7
	A prophecy given
	Luke 2:1-7
	A prophecy fulfilled
Carol:	Good Christian men, rejoice
Reading:	Luke 2:8-20
Choir:	Choral item
Reading:	Matthew 2:1-12,16-18
Carol:	Angels from the realms of glory
Prayers	
Carol:	Hark! the herald angels sing

Two
Meditations

It's good to plan some moments of reflective quietness into Christmas celebrations. Both of the following meditations may be used equally effectively by house groups or as part of a service.

'While they were there, the time came for the baby to be born, and she gave birth to her firstborn, a son. She wrapped him in cloths and placed him in a manger, because there was no room for them in the inn' (Luke 2:6,7).

Focal point: Place a candle beside a baby's carrycot or Moses basket.

There is something about a baby, Lord, which is quite unique,
Each one quite different from all others,
The colour of the hair, the shape of the eyes, the turn of the nose.
And yet within that uniqueness are traces of parenthood.
'He has his father's chin!',
'His mother's nose...',
'His grandfather's colouring...'

But there is something even more extraordinary about this baby, Lord.
God contracted to a span, incomprehensibly made man,
The Creator amongst his creation,
The Saviour amongst those whom he came to save,
Creative power concealed,
Divine glory hidden,
Deity invisible to an unsuspecting world,
Rejected, unwanted and unrecognized.
There was no room at the inn.

Forgive us, Lord, if today
We who live this side of Bethlehem, of Olivet and Calvary,
Turn away from the warmth and welcome of our lives
    The Creator
While we continue to abuse his creation;
    The Saviour
While we continue blind and oblivious of our need;
    Our God
While we worship the gods of our own creation,
Because we, too, fail to see the uniqueness of the Babe of Bethlehem. Amen.

'Do not be afraid. I bring you good news of great joy that will be for all the people' (Luke 2:10).

Focal point: Place a candle beside a selection of local and national newspapers.

There's never a shortage of news, Lord.
Every day there is enough news to fill the hungry columns of our
    newspapers,
The seconds and the minutes of our radios and televisions.
Never an apology for a shortage of news.

We are never short of sad news, Lord.
We grow accustomed with a numbing sense of acceptance to the
    sights of young children,
Their bodies wrecked through hunger, wracked with pain,
Gazing hopelessly into a future which is in reality no future at all.
We are rarely shocked, Lord, by the sights and the sounds of war,
Of people fleeing their bomb-scarred cities,
Of orphans bereaved of parents, or parents mourning the loss of
    life.
We have grown accustomed to such sights, Lord,
For sadness seems to be a constant part of today's news.

We are never short of bad news, Lord.
Thousands have lost their jobs, their livelihoods, their sense of
    fulfilment, their self-esteem and sense of worth.
They are statistics, Lord, often mere numbers, instead of people
Created by your hand and in your image.
Families have been divided, marriage vows broken,
Children's hearts become a battlefield in the fight for affection
    and justification.
We have grown accustomed to such sights, Lord,
For bad news seems to be a constant part of today's news.

We long for glad news, Lord.
News to thrill, to excite, to comfort and to encourage us.
But we are short of glad news, Lord.

And yet there is glad news, good news.
The angels declared it – good news of great joy for all people.
Good news!
God has broken into our world of sadness and evil with divine
    power,
To bring peace where there is hatred,
Reconciliation where there is division,
Fulfilment where there is frustration and failure,
Great joy where there is great sadness, silence and sorrow.

Help us this Christmas, dear Lord, amidst all the noises which
clamour for our attention, to be still, to hear the good news, to
find great joy and so to understand in reality the message of the
angels.

Amen.

THREE NATIVITY PLAYS

➤ *THE ANIMALS REMEMBER*

This nativity play for children is narrated by a cow and a donkey. They should be present, centre-stage, throughout. If you use masks, it's possible to have the animals' lines spoken by unseen readers.

Cast: Cow, donkey, 2 soldiers, Mary, Joseph, 3 innkeepers, Gabriel and angels, 4 shepherds, 3 wise men

Cow:	It's a lot quieter these days.
Donkey:	Yes, but I wonder how long it will last.
Cow:	Quite a long time, I should think. Thankfully, they don't have a census very often. Do you remember all those soldiers?
Donkey:	Yes, and all those foreign horses. I couldn't understand a thing they were neighing.
Cow:	It certainly caused quite a stir. People weren't very happy, were they? I can still remember when the soldiers first came. *(Pause while crowd assembles. Trumpet fanfare. Entry of the soldiers down church to the front. The soldiers stop at the front of the stage and face the congregation)*
Soldier 1:	Silence for the Emperor's messenger.
Soldier 2:	The Emperor decrees a census. *(Booing from the crowd)*
Soldier 1:	Silence. *(Draws sword)*
Soldier 2:	Every man will go to the town of his birth. No one is exempt. You must prepare now. The Emperor decrees it.
Soldiers:	Long live the Emperor! *(Soldiers march off. Enter Joseph and Mary)*
Joseph:	We can't possibly go while you are pregnant, Mary.
Mary:	Don't be silly, Joseph, you know we'll only get into trouble with the authorities. I'll be all right as long as we go slowly.
Joseph:	You're right, as usual. You can ride on the donkey but you must rest as soon as you feel tired.
Mary:	The donkey's very gentle. He always seems to know what is required. It's almost as if he can understand what we are saying. *(Joseph and Mary go to back of church)*

Donkey:	Of course I can understand what they are saying. They make me sound a right ass. It was a very long journey, though. Well over one hundred kilometres.
Cow:	You did a marvellous job.
Donkey:	Thank you, but the journey was easy compared with the noise and crowds of Bethlehem. Up and down, down and up the streets, looking for somewhere to stay.
	(Sing 'Little Donkey' while Joseph and Mary come down the aisle to the stage. Innkeepers mount the stage and a crowd enters around the stage. Joseph goes to first innkeeper)
Joseph:	Excuse me, but we need a room to stay in.
Innkeeper 1:	I'm sorry, but I can't help you. We're completely crowded out.
	(Joseph moves to second innkeeper)
Joseph:	My wife and I have just arrived and need somewhere to stay. Can you help?
Innkeeper 2:	I'd like to help, but it's impossible. We're full already. Try further along the High Street.
	(Joseph goes to the last innkeeper)
Joseph:	I must have a room for my wife. Our baby will be born very soon, surely you must have something?
Innkeeper 3:	A room I don't have, but I suppose you could stay in the stable. It's warm and dry and probably a lot quieter than inside.
Mary:	Thank you, it'll do just fine.
Innkeeper 3:	Come round the back and I'll show you where it is.
	(Mary and Joseph go off with innkeeper 3)
Cow:	And that's how we met.
Donkey:	It was nice to have someone to talk to after so long.
Cow:	Those sheep that turned up later had an interesting tale to tell, too.
	(Music while shepherds and sheep assemble. Song: 'Love shone down'. Gabriel enters at end of first chorus. Other angels enter and circle shepherds for last verse and chorus)
Gabriel:	Don't be afraid, shepherds. I have some good news for you. If you go to Bethlehem you will find a new-born baby who is your Saviour, Christ the Lord. You will find him in a stable lying in a manger. *(Angels leave)*
Shepherd 1:	Did you see what I saw or was I dreaming?
Shepherd 2:	No, we saw the angels too. Why do you think they came to us?
Shepherd 3:	I don't know, but I think we ought to go to Bethlehem and see the baby.
Shepherd 4:	Yes, but what about all our sheep? Won't they wander away?
Shepherd 2:	Or even get attacked by wolves?
Shepherd 4:	Or even lions?
Shepherd 3:	If God wants us to go to Bethlehem, then I'm sure he'll look after the sheep.
Shepherd 1:	You're right, let's go.
	(Exit shepherds hurriedly. Song: 'The Virgin Mary had a baby boy'. Enter Mary and Joseph; they sit either side of the manger peering into it. Shepherds enter)
Shepherd 2:	We have come to see the baby.
Shepherd 1:	Angels came and told us about him while we were in the fields with our sheep.
Shepherd 3:	Can we come in and see him, please?

Mary:	Of course you can, shepherds.
	(Shepherds crowd around manger)
Joseph:	We're glad you've come to share in our joy.
Shepherd 1:	Thank you for letting us see him but we'd better get back to our sheep.
Shepherd 2 and 3:	Yes, thank you.
	(Shepherds run off. Song: 'Lightly lift the stable bar'. Wise men enter and present gifts at the appropriate time in the verses)
Wise man 1:	We have travelled a long way to see this child.
Wise man 2:	The star told that a new, special king was to be born.
Wise man 3:	We have been following that star and it has led us to this child.
Wise man 2:	But we didn't expect to find him in a stable.
Wise man 1:	We know that he will turn the world upside down.
Donkey:	And soon after that they left, leaving me behind.
Cow:	That was because they had to leave in a hurry before Herod found the child and killed him.
Donkey:	You know, sometimes it just doesn't seem real. It all seems like a dream.
	(Song: 'Love shone down' including last verse)

Songs

'Little donkey', *Carol Gaily Carol*, A & C Black
'Love shone down', IQ Music
'The Virgin Mary had a baby boy', *Carols of Today*, Hodder and Stoughton
'Lightly lift the stable bar', *Carol Gaily Carol*, A & C Black

➤ AN 'INSTANT' NATIVITY PLAY

Nativity plays usually need weeks or months of preparation, fuss and bother – not this one! What's more, it gives adults the opportunity to take part in what is usually a children-only activity. It needs minimal preparation and the rehearsals are part of the celebration.

Scripts

On arrival everyone receives a copy of the script. Discourage pre-reading by rolling the scripts up and tying them like scrolls; give strict instructions not to open until told to do so.

Prepare twenty-two numbered scripts. These are for the 'principal actors'. Go through them in advance and mark up each character's lines with a highlighter. Judicious distribution of these by the sidespeople will ensure that reasonably confident and articulate people receive them. You can also add as many 'extra' characters (angels, shepherds, soldiers) as space at the front of the church permits.

Music

'Wake up' from Graham Kendrick's *Rumours of Angels* (Kingsway); 'Come and join the celebration' (*Mission Praise*).

Costumes and props

You will need: a simple crib; a suitable doll for the Christ child; bells, shakers, tambourines; a variety of head-dresses for instant identification – scarves for shepherds, tinsel for angels, a blue scarf for Mary, foil-covered plastic bowls for soldiers' helmets. If possible, try to find the following props: staff for Joseph to carry; large scroll for Zechariah; canes or broomsticks for soldiers; cardboard donkey and ox heads on a stick; bunch of hay for animals; cuddly toy lambs for shepherds; star on a stick; three gifts (two boxes and a jar). When the 'actors' speak their lines they should hold up their props to emphasize who they are. If you want to add to the spectacle you could have streamers and balloons at the end, but these are not necessary.

What to do

Introduce the concept of an instant nativity. Invite people to open their scripts. Practise the song. Divide the congregation into two groups: sheep (baa) and oxen (moo).

Adults with numbered scripts are the principal actors. Call on as many extras as you have props. Invite actors and extras to come forward and assemble in a line or semi-circle across the front of the church. Speed up the process of distributing props by numbering them in advance to match the numbered scripts.

Practise singing 'Come and join the celebration'. Rehearse the baas, moos, shaking of bells, etc. Show the actors how to step forward when it is their turn to speak. Have a brief practice involving several of the actors. Give the congregation a chance to practise their role as chorus. Make sure it is loud enough. Keep it all light and fun!

The script

Start with a roll on the drums or a trill on the piano.

Leader: Ladies and gentlemen, for the first time in living memory we present an instant nativity, celebrating Jesus' birthday.
Chorus: Wake up, wake up, it's Christmas morning.
Actor 1: I am the angel who brought Mary the news,
That the baby she bore would be King of the Jews.
Actor 2: I am the girl, who though meek and mild,
Agreed to look after God's wonderful child.
Actor 3: I am the carpenter, so skilled and so strong,
Who, puzzled and wondering, just went along.
Chorus: Wake up, wake up, it's Christmas morning.
Actor 4: I am the cousin, old Zach's wife,
When Mary arrived, my babe leapt to life.
Actor 5: I am Zechariah, whose voice was took
By an angel bright as I shivered and shook.
Actor 6: I am the soldier who counted the folk,
To add them all up was no kind of joke.
Chorus: Wake up, wake up, it's Christmas morning.
Actor 7: I am the donkey who carried the bride,
I may not be much, but I did it with pride.
Actors 8 & 9: And we are the innkeepers, her (him) and me,
A stable we gave them, but they had it for free.
Actor 10: I am the man who found them some hay,
To put in the manger, where the baby did lay.

Chorus:	Wake up, wake up, it's Christmas morning.
Actors 11 & 12:	We are the angels, a heavenly choir,
	Who startled the shepherds around the camp fire.
Actors 13 & 14:	Now shepherds we were, a-keeping our sheep,
	Some angels they came, and we got no more sleep.
Actors 15 & 16:	And we are the sheep, and we trotted far,
	To welcome the king with many a...
All:	... baaa.
Actors 17 & 18:	We are the oxen, who stood in the stall,
	Staying awake and just watching it all.
All:	Mooo, mooo, mooo, low, low, low.
Chorus:	Wake up, wake up, it's Christmas morning.
Actor 19:	And I am the star in the east so bright,
	Some travellers followed my guiding light.
Actors 20, 21 & 22:	We are three travellers, from lands afar,
	With frankincense, gold and some myrrh in a jar.
All actors:	We are the folk who have this good news to tell,
	God's Son has come, our Emmanuel.

(Song: 'Come and join the celebration') Actors process around church. If you want to add more activity, arm the congregation with party streamers and invite them to throw them as the procession passes. End the procession at the front with a great ring of bells / tambourines / trumpets. Encourage as much applause as possible.

➤ THE KING IN THE STABLE – AND IN THE GARAGE

This play is performed by two parallel sets of actors. Each set appears as required, going to different areas of the church or stage to form a Christmas tableau. There are no parts to be learned. Everyone listens to the narrators and moves accordingly. At the end there will be two tableaux – a traditional Christmas tableau and a contemporary version.

Cast: *Narrator 1, Mary, Joseph, innkeeper, shepherds, three wise men, King Herod.*
Narrator 2, Mary, Joseph, hostel manager, dustbin men, doctor, astronaut, rock star, Queen.

Narrator 1: The Roman emperor, Augustus, wanted to know how many people lived in his empire. Everyone had to go to the town where their family had come from to be registered. Joseph's family was from Bethlehem and so he and Mary had to travel there from Nazareth – eighty miles along very dusty roads. Mary was having a baby, so they borrowed a donkey. *(Enter Mary and Joseph – with or without donkey!)*

Narrator 2:	If Mary and Joseph had been living today they would probably only have been able to afford a bicycle for Mary. *(Enter Mary and Joseph – Mary riding on a bike)*
Narrator 1:	Arriving in Bethlehem, Joseph tried to find somewhere for them to stay the night. *(Joseph knocks on the inn door)*
Narrator 2:	Today they would probably have tried to find shelter in a small pub or hostel. *(Joseph knocks on the hostel door)*
Narrator 1:	The inn was full. But the innkeeper offered them his stable. *(Inn-keeper leads Mary and Joseph to the stable)*
Narrator 2:	Today he would probably have let them have his garage. *(Manager leads Mary and Joseph to garage)*
Narrator 1:	That night Mary's baby was born. It was a baby boy and she called him Jesus. She wrapped him up in the clothes she had brought with her from Nazareth and laid him on the straw in the cow's manger. *(Mary puts baby Jesus in the manger)*
Narrator 2:	Today Mary would probably have put her son in the basket of her bike. *(Mary puts baby Jesus in the bike basket)*
Narrator 1:	Outside in the fields were some shepherds. *(Enter shepherds at other side of stage)*
Narrator 2:	Today there may have been some bin men in the street outside nearby. *(Enter bin men)*
Narrator 1:	Suddenly the whole sky lit up! The shepherds and the bin men had to cover their eyes, the light was so bright. They were all very frightened. *(An angel appears)* The angel told the shepherds not to be frightened. He had good news for them. He told them that God's promised king had just been born in a stable nearby in Bethlehem. The angel told the shepherds to go and find the baby king asleep in a manger.
Narrator 2:	The angel told the bin men not to be frightened. He had some good news. He told them that God's promised king had just been born in a garage nearby in *(name of your town)*. He said, 'You will find the baby king asleep in a bike basket.' Then a lot more angels appeared, all singing praises to God. *(The angels leave)*
Narrator 1:	The shepherds found Mary and Joseph and the baby king. The baby was lying in a manger just like the angels had said. The shepherds knew that the angels had told them the truth. They knew that this baby was a very special person. The shepherds told Mary and Joseph all about the bright light and the angels and all about what the angels had told them about their baby, Jesus. *(The shepherds leave)*
Narrator 2:	The bin men found Mary and Joseph and the baby. He was in a bike basket just as the angels had said. The bin men knew that the angels had told them the truth and that this baby was a very special person. *(The bin men leave)*
Narrator 1:	They left the stable and went back to their sheep...
Narrator 2:	... and to their bins. They told everyone they met along the way about what had happened that night. *(Enter three wise men)*
Narrator 1:	Three people from another land had been following an unusual star, convinced that it meant that an important birth had taken place. *(Three wise men set off following the star)*
Narrator 2:	Three VIPs had been to an international conference. One was an astronaut, another was a doctor and the third was a rock star. They heard rumours that someone very important had just been

born. They agreed they should try to find this baby.

Narrator 1: The three wise men arrived in Jerusalem and went straight to the king's palace. *(Three wise men approach Herod)*

Narrator 2: The VIPs arrived in London and went straight to Buckingham Palace as they thought that a new king would be born in a palace. *(The VIPs approach the Queen)*

Narrator 1: They asked Herod where they might find the new baby king. Herod was angry. He didn't want another king in his land. But he pretended to be pleased to see them. *(Herod smiles at the three wise men)*

Narrator 2: The Queen was very polite, but knew nothing of a new addition to the royal family.

Narrator 1: King Herod told the three wise men that he, too, wanted to see the new baby king. He begged them to return to him with news of this remarkable child. But he wasn't telling the truth. He really wanted to kill the baby. They left Herod and followed the star from Jerusalem to Bethlehem where the star stopped over the stable.

Narrator 2: The VIPs, too, found their way to the backstreet garage in *(name of your town)*.

Narrator 1: The wise men gave expensive presents to the baby Jesus. One of them had brought some gold.

Narrator 2: The VIPs had brought expensive presents for the baby Jesus. The astronaut had brought some moon rock.

Narrator 1: Another wise man had brought some special ointment called myrrh.

Narrator 2: The doctor had brought some special medicine.

Narrator 1: The third wise man had brought some sweet-smelling frankincense for Jesus.

Narrator 2: The rock star had brought his latest CD for Jesus.

Narrator 1: The three wise men left Mary and Joseph and went back home. They did not go and tell King Herod where the baby king was because God had warned them in a dream not to tell him.

Narrator 2: The VIPs left Mary and Joseph and went back home.

Narrator 1: Mary was very puzzled by what was going on...

Narrator 2: ... but she knew that God had told her that her baby would be a very special baby and so she never forgot these visitors and these gifts. *(Shepherds, bin men, wise men and VIPs return and make a tableau round Mary and Joseph and Jesus)*

Appropriate songs or carols can be interspersed as required.

READINGS AND PRAYERS

➤ *A FAMILY ACT OF PRAYER*

The text of this simple act of prayer can be adapted for more, or fewer, than five voices. The second part may be reproduced as an OHP slide so that the congregation may join in the responses.

Reader 1:	Thank you, Jesus, for coming.
Reader 2:	Thank you for coming to earth to be born in a stable.
Reader 3:	Thank you for your life on earth.
Reader 4:	Thank you for dying on a cross for us...
Reader 5:	... and for rising again to new life for us.
All:	And for being here with us today.
Reader 1:	Thank you for all the presents we have received today. Thank you for families and for fun.
Reader 2:	We pray for people who have no presents this Christmas, for the poor and the lonely.
Reader 3:	We pray for people who live in places where there is war and fighting.
Reader 4:	We pray for people who have no home.
Reader 5:	And we pray for those who don't know you and don't understand the real meaning of Christmas.
All:	May the light of Jesus shine in all our lives.
Reader 1:	Please help us to be more like Jesus.
Reader 2:	Help us to share your good gifts with others.
Reader 3:	Help us to tell others the good news about you and how you came to save us.
Reader 4:	Help us to live our lives in obedience to you.
Reader 5:	Let us praise God together. Let us worship the Saviour.
Reader 1:	Heavenly King, yet born of Mary. Jesus, Son of God...
Congregation:	... we praise and adore you.
Reader 2:	Eternal Word, yet child without speech. Jesus,

	Son of God...
Congregation:	... we praise and adore you.
Reader 3:	Robed in glory, yet wrapped in infant clothes. Jesus, Son of God...
Congregation:	... we praise and adore you.
Reader 4:	Lord of heaven and earth, yet sleeping in a manger. Jesus, Son of God...
All:	... we praise and adore you. To you, Jesus, Strong in your weakness, Glorious in your humility, Mighty to save, Be all praise and glory with the Father and the Holy Spirit, Now and for ever. Amen.

➤ WHAT'S IT ALL ABOUT?

Choral speech for children aged between nine and twelve. Divide the main group into two sections.

All:	What's it all about? *(Gradually become louder and faster)* What is it? What is it? What is it? What is it? What is it all about?
Group A:	Thinking
Group B:	Wondering
Group A:	Rushing
Group B:	Shopping
Group A:	Crowding
Group B:	Jostling
Group A:	Pushing
Group B:	Shoving
Group A:	Queuing
Group B:	Waiting
Group A:	Thinking
Group B:	... and wondering
All:	What is it about?
Group A:	Listing
Group B:	Shopping
Group A:	Choosing
Group B:	Wondering
Group A:	Something for Mum
Group B:	... and Dad
Group A:	Something for aunt
Group B:	Uncle and nephew
Group A:	Something for Grandad

Group B:	(Sadly) Two years since Gran died
Group A:	Something for those
Group B:	... who gave to us last year
Group A:	Thinking
Group B:	... and wondering
All:	What is it about?
Group A:	Cooking, preparing
Group B:	Stuffing the turkey
Group A:	Scrubbing potatoes
Group B:	Cutting the parsnips
Group A:	Topping the sprouts
Group B:	And boiling the peas
Group A:	Heating the pudding
Group B:	Stirring the custard
Group A:	Laying the table
Group B:	Checking the turkey
Group A:	Thinking
Group B:	... and wondering
All:	What is it about?
Group A:	Sitting and eating
Group B:	Stuffing and gorging
Group A:	Pulling the crackers
Group B:	Cracking the jokes
Group A:	Wearing strange hats
Group B:	Laughing and talking
Group A:	Sitting and watching
Group B:	Sleeping and snoring
Group A:	Bring out the bottle
Group B:	Fill up the glasses
Group A:	Arguing, bickering
Group B:	Rowing and fighting
Group A:	Thinking
Group B:	... and wondering
All:	What is it about?
Group A:	Tired and irritable
Group B:	End of the day
Group A:	Washing the dishes
Group B:	Putting away
Group A:	Gathering the litter
Group B:	Straightening the chairs
Group A:	Checking the damage
Group B:	Removing the stains
Group A:	Missing the laughter
Group B:	The jokes and the friends
Group A:	Bolting the door
Group B:	And climbing the stairs
Group A:	Thinking
Group B:	... and wondering
Group A:	Thinking
Group B:	... and wondering
Group A:	Thinking
Group B:	... and wondering
All:	What is it about?

➤ CHRISTMAS CRIB READINGS

The readings and prayers outlined here are for use at home or in church as figures are added one by one to a manger scene. They are most effective when used with a set of crib figures, but will work with flannelgraph pictures on a board too. Their origins are a long-standing family custom we have kept in the days running up to Christmas. We use a set of simple home-made figures. After lighting a candle, we read the day's passage and add the appropriate figure to the manger. One of the family says a prayer and we sing a verse or two of a carol. The following outline was written for a young people's carol service at which members of the congregation brought the crib figures to the front. It can be adapted for a Christmas Eve crib service, or used for a series of school assemblies.

1. Mary

Reading: Luke 1:26-38
Prayer: Heavenly Father, you prepared for the coming of your Son into the world by calling Mary to be his mother. Thank you for her example of humility and obedience and for the care she showed in his upbringing. Help us to welcome his coming with great joy as she did. May our homes be places where Jesus is always welcome, for his name's sake. Amen.

2. Joseph

Reading: Matthew 1:18-25
Prayer: We thank you, Lord God, that the angel who visited Joseph found he was willing to follow your way. Help us to learn to obey and serve you, even when it may be hard and lead to ridicule and scorn. We pray that we may acknowledge your Son as Jesus our Saviour, and as Emmanuel, God with us. We ask it in his name. Amen.

3. The manger

Reading: Luke 2:1-7
Prayer: We praise you, loving God, for sending your very own Son into our world. We wonder at his willingness to lay aside all the splendour of heaven, which was his by right, in order to be born as a helpless baby. Although there was no room at the inn, may we welcome Jesus into our hearts and homes this Christmas time. May we discover the joy and peace his presence brings. We ask this through Christ our Lord. Amen.

4. Angels

Reading: Luke 2:8-14
Prayer: With the angels we give glory to you, Lord God, that the coming of Jesus is a message bringing good news. We give thanks that Christ the Lord has been born in Bethlehem as our Saviour. Help us to discover the peace with you that he came to bring. We pray too for peace in our world this Christmas, for the glory of your name. Amen.

5. The shepherds

Reading: Luke 2:15-20

Prayer: Gracious God, the fact that the birth of your Son was announced first of all to ordinary shepherds encourages us to turn to him also. May we rejoice like them in discovering the truth of the message that Jesus is our Saviour, and may we share the message about him with those we meet. In his name we pray. Amen.

6. The wise men

Reading: Matthew 2:1-12

Prayer: Thank you, Father, for guiding the wise men by the light of the star to the place where they found Jesus, your Son. With them we worship and adore him as our king. Help us to offer him our gifts, above all the gifts of our love and of the obedience of our lives, for the glory of his name. Amen.

7. The baby Jesus

Reading: John 1:1-14 or John 1:1-5,14

Prayer: Almighty God, we can never fully understand how your Son became a human being and lived among us, bringing your light into a world made dark by our disobedience and sin. Help us to welcome him and so become your very own children. May this Christmas Day be a real celebration of his birthday as we praise you for the birth of your Son, Jesus, in whose name we pray. Amen.

SKELETON SERMONS

➤ *TALKS FOR ADVENT, CHRISTMAS AND EPIPHANY*

What follows is a selection of brief talk outlines – simply the skeleton of the talk giving you the opportunity to flesh it out in your own style.

Advent Family Service
Mark 1:1-8

Prepare the way of the Lord!

- ○ *What do you want for Xmas?*
  Anyone want an earth mover – to get the road ready?
- ○ One part of John the Baptist's message was: **'get the road ready'.**
  Repent – turn away from your sins.
- ○ What earth needs moving in us?
  Our sins over the last year, or in the pre-Christmas rush?
- ○ Children's sins – adult sins.
- ○ Other part of the 'get ready' message:
  Make the road straight.
- ○ The king is coming down that road, so it's got to go the right way. Line it up – by looking to the one who's coming.
- ○ **Who?** Not just a baby – 'mightier than'.
- ○ **Where?** Not just a manger – 'to my life'.
- ○ **What?** Not just good feelings – 'baptism of the Holy Spirit'.

Christmas Midnight Service
Luke 2:1-4
John 1:1-14

Is it for real?

- ○ A child says: 'Santa's coming at midnight. You'll be in church, won't you? You might see him.' Next year he won't believe in Santa – will he soon give up believing in Jesus too?
- ○ How many of us say 'Christmas is for kids' because we think of it as we do about Santa Claus – a lovely story, but not true. Even we who come to church? Do we come to enjoy the lovely story, and wish, wistfully, that it was true?
- ○ Mind you, it *is* a lovely story – a lovely idea. Glory to God, peace on Earth.
- ○ God's love stoops down and plants a kiss on earth – could it be real?

○ Light in darkness. Darkness could not put it out. Could it be real?

○ A holy family – in a society where we have to go outside the family for support, for a listening ear. They faced so much together – could it be for real?

○ I'm here to tell you it is real. How do I know?

○ *History* 'The Word became flesh' – idea became a real man. The story is full of real pain, real dirt as well.

○ *Our experience* 'We have seen his glory.' Our story is real, too, living out Jesus' life in the 1990s. It involves joy and pain – and shame when we let him down.

○ We're not perfect – but our 'Jesus story' is real. It has lasted since last Christmas and will last through the year ahead. This is not because we are good in ourselves. We're only able to be called Christians because Jesus, born in a stable in Palestine, now lives in and among his people.

○ His love, his strength flow through us, making the story real today.

Epiphany Family Service
Isaiah 49:1-6
Matthew 2:1-12

Our gifts to Jesus the Lord

○ **Wise men gave gifts.** They knew little of Jesus.
What about us? We know Jesus – so can we offer less?
We can only give what we have already received.
God wants to give to us – we come with empty hands.
And what we do have (given by God), he wants us to give back to him.
Offer yourselves as a living sacrifice and as part of that, offer your gold, frankincense and myrrh.

○ **Gold** – pure, beautiful, fit for a king. Work for it. Will you pass off small change to the Almighty? Giving of one's best to God is a response of faith and of obedience. We say he's the best – we give our best. We put our money where our mouth is.

○ **Frankincense** – was used in worship. It's not useful in itself. When we 'waste' time and effort in prayer, God gives back more than he receives. He longs for us to make the first move with a personal offering, a sacrifice of praise.

○ **Myrrh** – is bitter. It was used in preparing bodies for burial. A strange present for a small child. Have you any not-very-nice presents for the Lord Jesus? Bitter feelings, bitter experiences? Offer them to the Lord as well. He will accept them and will either gradually heal them or transform them.

■ Reference Booklist

Resources from CPAS

CPAS Catalogue code	Title	Author and publisher
03168	The Dramatised Bible	Bible Society / Marshall Pickering
00280	The First Christmas	Lion Publishing (Children's Video Bible)
92420	Celebrating the Festivals	Sue Kirby, CPAS
92424	Making the Festivals Fun	Sue Kirby, CPAS
82003	Creating a Church for the Unchurched	Anne Hibbert, CPAS
	Church Leadership Pack &	
	Church Leadership Video	Contact CPAS for subscription information

Carols

Carols for Today	Jubilate, Hodder and Stoughton
Carol Praise	Jubilate, Hodder and Stoughton
Carolling	Jubilate, Hodder and Stoughton
Play Carol Praise	Jubilate, Hodder and Stoughton

■ Acknowledgements

Building Bridges: Ida Glaser
Stir-up Sunday: Peter Dowman
Skeleton Sermons: Chris Burch
Readings and Prayers: Mark Smith; Geoff Treasure; Brian Parfitt
Out and About: Derek Williams *(Shoppers' Carol Service)*; Mark Smith *(Opening Time)*; Jill Harris *(Hold the Front Page)*; John Fryer *(School Assemblies)*
Three Nativity Plays: Mike Wheeler *(The Animals Remember)*; John and Angela Haynes *(Instant Nativity)*; Christine Holmes *(The King in the Stable – and in the Garage)*
Two Meditations: Geoff Treasure
Family Service Talks: James Ambrose *(A Piece of Straw)*; Tony Butterworth *(Unwrapping God's Present)*; Roland Heaney *(Don't Miss Out!)*, Mark Smith *(Present Tense?)*
Celebrating with Young Children: Rachel Heathfield; Steve Pierce *(Jesse Tree)*
A Carol Service: Steve Pierce
A Talk for Adults: David Lewthwaite
A Seeker-friendly Christmas: Tony Eccleston and Dave Trimmingham of Led Free Theatre Company, Southcourt Baptist Church, Aylesbury *(The Meaning of Christmas* and *Covert Operations)*; Steve Tilley *(Lads)*

Copyright © 1996 CPAS
Published by
Church Pastoral Aid Society
Athena Drive
Tachbrook Park
WARWICK
CV34 6NG

Telephone: (01926) 334242
Orderline: (01926) 335855
Fax: (01926) 337613
Registered Charity No 1007820
A company limited by guarantee

First edition 1996
ISBN 1 8976 6063 4

Illustrations by Doug Hewitt
Editorial and design by AD Publishing Services Ltd

Printed by Unigraph Printing Services, Sheffield

British Library Cataloguing-in-Publication Data. A Catalogue record for this book is available from the British Library.